MATHEMATICS

THE STUDY OF NUMBERS, QUANTITY, AND SPACE

MATHEMATICS

THE STUDY OF NUMBERS, QUANTITY, AND SPACE

EDITED BY TRACEY BAPTISTE

Britannica
Educational Publishing

IN ASSOCIATION WITH

ROSEN
EDUCATIONAL SERVICES

Published in 2015 by Britannica Educational Publishing (a trademark of Encyclopædia Britannica, Inc.) in association with The Rosen Publishing Group, Inc.
29 East 21st Street, New York, NY 10010

Distributed exclusively by Rosen Publishing.
To see additional Britannica Educational Publishing titles, go to rosenpublishing.com.

First Edition

Britannica Educational Publishing
J. E. Luebering: Director, Core Reference Group
Anthony L. Green: Editor, Compton's by Britannica

Rosen Publishing
Hope Lourie Killcoyne: Executive Editor
Tracey Baptiste: Editor
Nelson Sá: Art Director
Michael Moy: Designer
Cindy Reiman: Photography Manager
Introduction and supplementary material: Mindy Hauser

Cataloging-in-Publication Data

Mathematics: the study of numbers, quantity, and space/edited by Tracey Baptiste.
       pages cm.—(The story of math: core principles of mathematics)
Includes bibliographical references and index.
ISBN 978-1-62275-530-1 (library bound)
1. Mathematics—History—Juvenile literature. I. Baptiste, Tracey, editor. II. Title: Study of numbers, quantity, and space.
QA141.3.M352 2015
510.9—dc23

                                                                              2014023252

Manufactured in the United States of America

Photo credits: Cover and interior pages agsandrew/Shutterstock.com; cover, p. 3 (top) Indivision 07 Grow B/Getty Images.

Contents

Introduction

I n the grocery store, the shopper is trying to figure out the cheapest way to purchase corn chips. The 6-ounce bag costs $6. The 3-ounce bag costs $3.50. Should the shopper purchase two 3-ounce bags or buy one 6-ounce bag?

On the baseball field, the batter is calculating his batting average after every pitch. The architect has to figure out the volume of water that fits inside a bathtub before she can design a support for it. The caterer is trying to estimate how many people in a party of 100 will prefer to have the chicken dish or the vegetable.

Welcome to the study of numbers, quantity, and space, also known as mathematics. Mathematics is much more than a class at school. Math is everywhere and is used by people dozens of times a day. People use math to figure out how much time they have in the morning before work or school. They use math when purchasing products, doing home repairs, and cooking dinner. Math helps people recognize patterns and understand the world around them.

People who major in math in college do not just become math teachers. Mathematicians work in every area of society. They work for big

The arc made by a ball thrown in the air is a parabola. David Madison/
Photographer's Choice/Getty Images

businesses and industries. They are employed at all levels of government. They work at universities. Mathematicians may be accountants, work in the insurance industry, work at nonprofits, or become market researchers, analysts, financial advisers, real estate agents, and statisticians. They may go on to become doctors, lawyers, architects, scientists, computer programmers, video game developers, digital animators, and more.

That's because mathematicians learn how to use logic and analysis. In many ways, math is a language that first developed in the ancient world. And like a language, math has continued to evolve and grow.

The Egyptians show evidence of math through their man-made pyramids. The Babylonians of ancient Mesopotamia developed ways to work with fractions. The Greeks took math to a philosophical level, using it for reasoning.

Indian mathematicians advanced algebra. Italians, during the Renaissance, began using letters of the alphabet in algebraic equations.

In the 17th century, calculus and analytic geometry were developed. Isaac Newton, an English physicist who is considered one of the most influential scientists of all time, used both physics and math to make many mathematical discoveries.

The 18th and 19th centuries saw tremendous changes in mathematics and more specialization by German, English, French, and United States mathematicians.

Today, mathematics is highly specialized. There are many subdivisions of modern mathematics, including algebra, calculus, geometry, and trigonometry. There is complex analysis, the branch of math that investigates complex numbers; number theory, the study of different number systems; set theory, the expression of mathematics in terms of sets; and mathematical logic, drawing conclusions from premises.

Math will continue to evolve and grow. Think about how computers have changed the way math is studied. Mathematicians now use computers to solve problems too difficult to solve on paper.

To understand where math is today, it's important to start at the beginning.

Chapter 1

MATHEMATICS IN THE ANCIENT WORLD

Mathematics is often defined as the study of quantity, magnitude, and relations of numbers or symbols. It embraces the subjects of arithmetic, geometry, algebra, calculus, probability, statistics, and many other special areas of research.

There are two major divisions of mathematics: pure and applied. Pure mathematics investigates the subject solely for its theoretical interest. Applied mathematics develops tools and techniques for solving specific problems of business and engineering or for highly theoretical applications in the sciences.

Mathematics is pervasive throughout modern life. Baking a cake or building a house involves the use of numbers, geometry, measures, and space. The design of precision instruments, the development of new technologies, and advanced computers all use more technical mathematics.

Mathematics first arose from the practical need to measure time and to count. Thus, the history of mathematics begins with the origins of numbers and recognition of the dimensions and properties of space and time. The earliest evidence of primitive forms of counting occurs in notched bones and scored pieces of wood and stone. Early uses of geometry are revealed in patterns found on ancient cave walls and pottery.

EGYPT AND MESOPOTAMIA

As civilizations arose in Asia and the Near East, the field of mathematics evolved. Both sophisticated number systems and basic knowledge of arithmetic, geometry, and algebra began to develop.

The earliest continuous records of mathematical activity that have survived in written form are from the 2nd millennium BCE. The Egyptian pyramids reveal evidence of a fundamental knowledge of surveying and geometry as early as 2900 BCE. Written testimony of what the Egyptians knew, however, is known from documents drawn up about 1,000 years later.

Two of the best-known sources for our current knowledge of ancient Egyptian

The three pyramids at Giza line up within three-sixtieths of a degree of true north-south. Space Imaging Europe/Photo Researchers, Inc./ Science Source

mathematics are the Rhind papyrus and the Moscow papyrus. These present many different kinds of practical mathematical problems, including applications to surveying, salary distributions, calculations of the areas of simple geometric surfaces and volumes such as the truncated pyramid, and simple solutions for first- and second-degree equations.

COMPARISON OF NUMERALS IN THE BASE-TEN AND BASE-TWO SYSTEMS

NUMERALS			Base-Two
Base-Ten	Base-Two		Base-Two
0	0_{two}	$= [0 \times (1)] = 0$	0_{two}
1	1_{two}	$= [1 \times (1)] = 1$	1_{two}
2	10_{two}	$= [1 \times (2)] + [0 \times (1)] = 2$	10_{two}
3	11_{two}	$= [1 \times (2)] + [1 \times (1)] = 2 + 1 = 3$	11_{two}
4	100_{two}	$= [1 \times (2 \times 2)] + [0 \times (2)] + [0 \times (1)] = 4 + 0 + 0 = 4$	100_{two}
7	111_{two}	$= [1 \times (2 \times 2)] + [1 \times (2)] + [1 \times (1)] = 4 + 2 + 1 = 7$	111_{two}
8	1000_{two}	$= [1 \times (2 \times 2 \times 2)] + [0 \times (2 \times 2)] + [0 \times (2)] + [0 \times (1)] = 8$	1000_{two}
16	10000_{two}	$= [1 \times (2 \times 2 \times 2 \times 2)] + 0 + 0 + 0 + 0 = 16$	10000_{two}
19	10011_{two}	$= [1 \times (2 \times 2 \times 2 \times 2)] + 0 + 0 + [1 \times (2)] + [1 \times (1)] = 16 + 0 + 0 + 2 + 1 = 19$	10011_{two}

The simplicity of the binary system makes it ideal for use in computing. Encyclopædia Britannica, Inc.

Egyptian arithmetic, based on counting in groups of 10, was relatively simple. Base-10 systems, the most widespread throughout the world, probably arose for biological reasons. The fingers of both hands facilitated natural counting in groups of 10. Numbers are sometimes called digits from the Latin word for finger. In the Egyptians' base-10 arithmetic, hieroglyphs stood for individual units and groups of tens, hundreds, and thousands. Higher powers of 10 made it possible to count numbers into the millions. Unlike our familiar number system, which is both decimal and positional (23 is not the same as 32), the Egyptians' arithmetic was not positional but additive.

Unlike the Egyptians, the Babylonians of ancient Mesopotamia developed flexible techniques for dealing with fractions. They also succeeded in developing a more sophisticated base-10 arithmetic that was positional, and they kept mathematical records on clay tablets. The most remarkable feature of Babylonian arithmetic was its use of a sexagesimal (base 60) place-valued system in addition to a decimal system. Thus the Babylonians counted in groups of 60 as well as 10. Babylonian mathematics is still used to tell time—an hour consists of 60 minutes, and each minute is divided into 60 seconds—and circles are measured in divisions of 360 degrees.

The Babylonians apparently adopted their base-60 number system for economic reasons. Their principal units of weight and money were the mina, consisting of 60 shekels, and the talent, consisting of 60 mina. This sexagesimal arithmetic was used in commerce and astronomy. Surviving tablets also show the Babylonians' facility in computing compound interest, squares, and square roots.

Because their base-60 system was especially flexible for computation and handling fractions, the Babylonians were particularly strong in algebra and number theory. Tablets survive giving solutions to first-, second-, and some third-degree equations. Despite rudimentary knowledge of geometry, the Babylonians knew many cases of the Pythagorean theorem for right triangles. They also knew accurate area formulas for triangles and trapezoids. Since they used a crude approximation of three for the value of pi, they achieved only rough estimates for the areas of circles.

PYTHAGOREAN THEOREM

Pythagorean theorem, proposition number 47 from Book I of Euclid's *Elements of Geometry*, is the well-known geometric theorem that the sum of the squares on the legs of a right triangle is equal to the square on the hypotenuse (the side opposite the right angle)—or, in familiar algebraic notation, $a^2 + b^2 = c^2$. Although the theorem has long been associated with the Greek mathematician–philosopher Pythagoras (c. 580–500 BCE), it is actually far older. Four Babylonian tablets, circa 1900–1600 BCE, indicate some knowledge of the theorem or at least of special integers known as Pythagorean triples that satisfy it. Similarly, the Rhind papyrus, dating from about 1650 BCE but known to be a copy of a 200-year-old document, indicates that the Egyptians knew about the theorem.

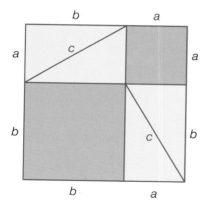 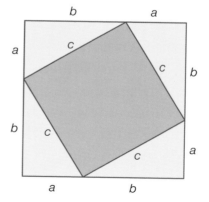

This visual proof of the Pythagorean theorem may be the original proof that states that the sum of the squares on the sides of a right triangle equals the square on the hypotenuse. Encyclopædia Britannica, Inc.

GREECE AND ROME

The Greeks were the first to develop a truly mathematical spirit. They were interested not only in the applications of mathematics but in its philosophical significance, which was especially appreciated by Plato.

The Greeks developed the idea of using mathematical formulas to prove the validity

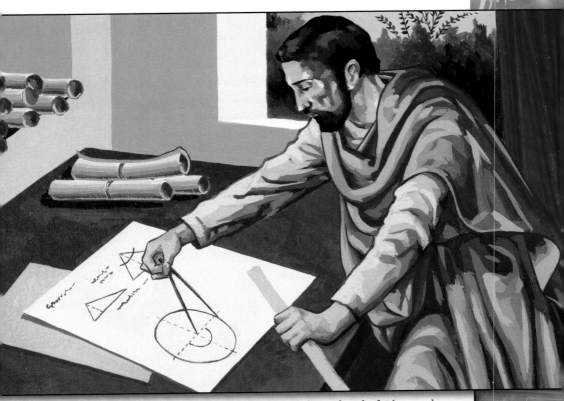

Euclid was a Greek mathematician who founded the School of Alexandria.
Universal Images Group/Getty Images

17

of a proposition. Some Greeks, like Aristotle, engaged in the theoretical study of logic, the analysis of correct reasoning. No previous mathematics had dealt with abstract entities or the idea of a mathematical proof.

Pythagoras provided one of the first proofs in mathematics and discovered incommensurable magnitudes, or irrational numbers. The Pythagorean theorem relates the sides of a right triangle with their corresponding squares. The discovery of irrational magnitudes had another consequence for the Greeks: Since the lengths of diagonals of squares could not be expressed by rational numbers of the form a/b, the Greek number system was inadequate for describing them. Due to the incompleteness of their number system, the Greeks developed geometry at the expense of algebra. The only systematic contribution to algebra was made much later in antiquity by Diophantus. Called the father of algebra, he devised symbols to represent operations, unknown quantities, and frequently occurring constants.

Ancient knowledge of the sciences was often wrong and wholly unsatisfactory by modern standards. However, the mathematics of Euclid, Apollonius of Perga, and Archimedes—the three greatest

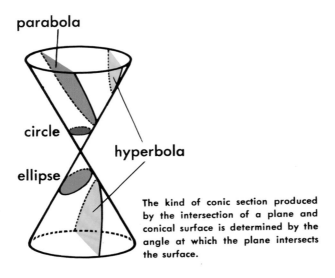

parabola

circle

hyperbola

ellipse

The kind of conic section produced by the intersection of a plane and conical surface is determined by the angle at which the plane intersects the surface.

The conic sections are produced by the intersection of a plane and a right circular cone. Depending on the angle of the plane relative to the cone, a circle, an ellipse, a parabola, or a hyperbola is produced. Encyclopædia Britannica, Inc.

mathematicians of antiquity—remains as valid today as it was more than 2,000 years ago. Euclid's *Elements of Geometry* used logic and deductive reasoning to set up axioms, postulates, and a collection of theorems related to plane and solid geometry, as well as a theory of proportions used to resolve the difficulty of irrational numbers. Despite its flaws, the *Elements* remains a historic example of how to establish universally agreed-upon knowledge by following a rigorous course of deductive logic. Apollonius, best known for his work on conic sections, coined the terms *parabola*, *hyperbola*, and *ellipse*. Another great figure was Ptolemy, who contributed to the development of trigonometry and mathematical astronomy.

Roman mathematicians, in contrast to the Greeks, are renowned for being very practical. The Roman mind did not favor the abstract side of mathematics, which had so delighted the Greeks. The Romans cared instead for the usefulness of mathematics in measuring and counting. As the fortunes of the Roman Empire declined, a rising interest in mathematics developed elsewhere, in India and among Arab scholars.

MATHEMATICS IN THE MIDDLE AGES AND RENAISSANCE

Ancient Greek and Roman mathematicians influenced those in the Arab world, who went on to advance the study of algebra. Arabic mathematical theory was widely adopted and influenced the work of European, and then American, mathematicians. As a result, the Middle Ages and Renaissance periods saw innovations in thinking and theory that led to the widespread use of symbolic algebra and the invention of the calculus.

MATHEMATICS IN INDIA AND THE ARAB WORLD

Indian mathematicians were especially skilled in arithmetic, methods of calculation, algebra, and trigonometry. Aryabhata calculated pi to a very accurate value of 3.1416, and Brahmagupta and Bhaskara II advanced the study of indeterminate equations. Because Indian mathematicians were not concerned with such theoretical problems as irrational numbers, they were able to make great strides in algebra. Their decimal place-valued number system, including zero, was especially suited for easy calculation. Indian mathematicians, however, lacked interest in a sense of proof. Most of their results were presented simply as useful techniques for given situations, especially in astronomical or astrological computations.

A statue of Aryabhata stands in the Inter University Centre for Astronomy and Astrophysics in Pune, India. Mukerjee

One of the greatest scientific minds of Islam was al-Khwarizmi, who worked at the "House of Wisdom" translating scientific and philosophic treatises, particularly Greek. He also published his own original research. Arab mathematicians translated and commented on Ptolemy's astronomy before it was brought to the attention of Europeans. Islamic scholars not only translated the works of Euclid, Archimedes, Apollonius, and Ptolemy into Arabic but advanced beyond what the Greek mathematicians had done to provide new results of their own.

Muhammad ibn Musa al-Khwarizmi, a Persian mathematician, was responsible for going beyond the work of Greek mathematicians and giving us the word algebra. De Agostini/C. Sappa/Getty Images

By the end of the 8th century the influence of Islam had extended as far west as Spain. It was there, primarily, that Arabic, Jewish, and Western scholars eventually translated Greek and Islamic manuscripts

WHY ALGEBRA IS CALLED ALGEBRA

We can thank mathematician al–Khwarizmi (c. 780–850) for the words *algebra* and *algorithm*. The Muslim mathematician and astronomer introduced Hindu–Arabic numerals and the concepts of algebra into European mathematics. His work on elementary algebra, called *al–Kitāb al–mukhtaṣar fī ḥisāb al–jabr wa'l–muqābala* is where we get the word *algebra* (*al–jabr*). A second work, titled *Algoritmi de numero Indorum*, introduced Hindu–Arabic numerals and gives us the word *algorithm*.

into Latin. By the 13th century, original mathematical work by European authors had begun to appear.

RENAISSANCE PERIOD

Most of the early mathematical activity of the Renaissance was centered in Italy, where the mathematician Luca Pacioli wrote a standard text on arithmetic, algebra, and geometry that served to introduce the subject to students for generations. The solution of the cubic equation instigated great rivalries and priority claims between Italian mathematicians Scipione del Ferro, Niccolò Tartaglia, and

Gerolamo Cardano. Among the advances in algebra made during the 16th century, the use of letters of the alphabet to denote constants, variables, and unknowns in equations is notable. This symbolic algebra later proved to be the key to advances in geometry, algebra, and the infinitesimal calculus.

17TH CENTURY

Mathematics received considerable stimulus in the 17th century from astronomical problems.

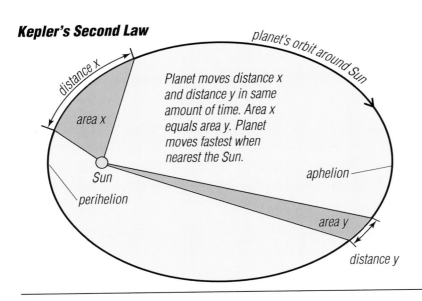

Kepler's Second Law

planet's orbit around Sun

distance x

area x

Planet moves distance x and distance y in same amount of time. Area x equals area y. Planet moves fastest when nearest the Sun.

Sun

perihelion

aphelion

area y

distance y

Kepler's second law of planetary motion describes the speed of a planet traveling in an elliptical orbit around the Sun. It states that a line between the Sun and the planet sweeps equal areas in equal times. Encyclopædia Britannica, Inc.

The astronomer Johannes Kepler, for example, who discovered the elliptical shape of the planetary orbits, was especially interested in the problem of determining areas bounded by curved figures. Kepler and other mathematicians used infinitesimal methods of one sort or another to find a general solution for the problem of areas. In connection with such questions, the French mathematician Pierre de Fermat investigated properties of maxima and minima. He also discovered a method of determining tangents to curves, a problem closely related to the almost simultaneous development of the differential and integral calculus by Isaac Newton and Gottfried Wilhelm Leibniz later in the century.

Of equal importance to the invention of the calculus was the independent discovery of analytic geometry by Fermat and René Descartes. Of the two, Descartes used a better notation and devised superior techniques. Above all, he showed how the solution of simultaneous equations was facilitated through the application of analytic geometry. Many geometric problems could be translated directly into equivalent algebraic terms for solution.

Developed in the 17th century, projective geometry involves, in part, the analysis of

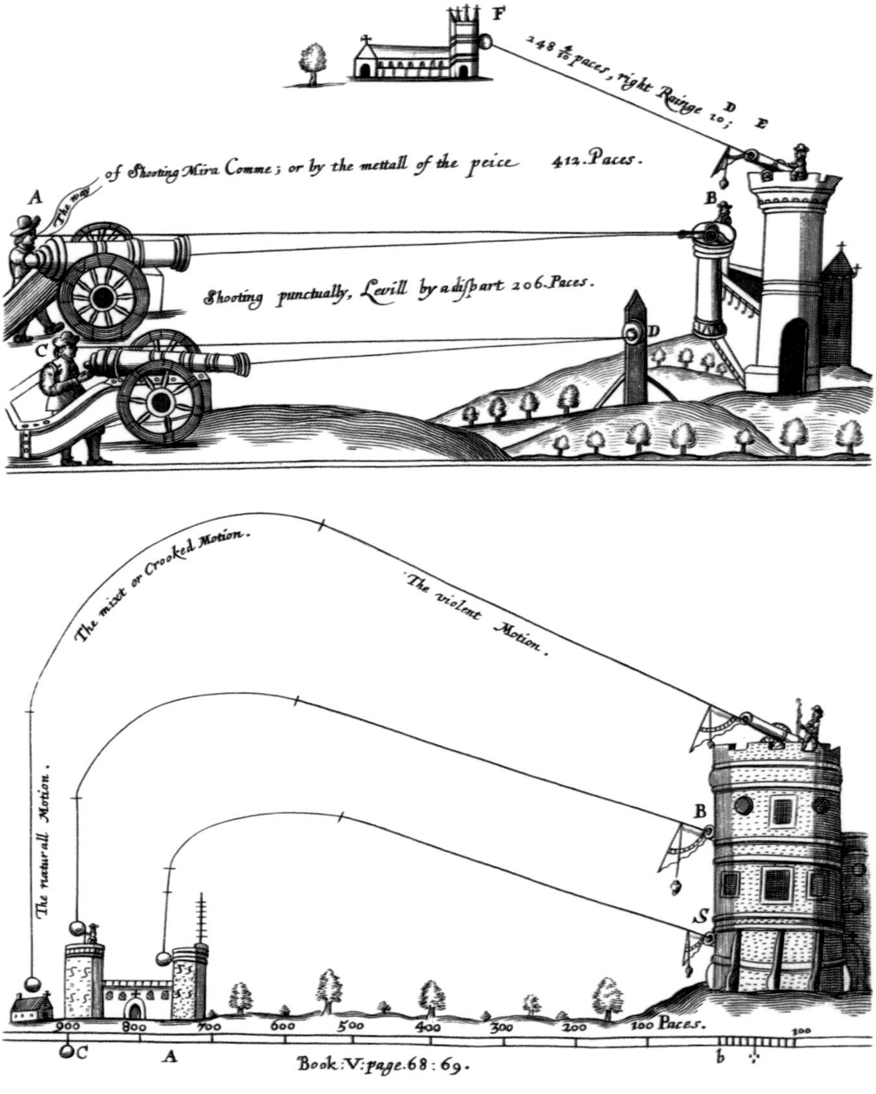
F
paces, right Raige 20;
D
E
The way of Shooting Mira Comme; or by the mettall of the peice 412. Paces.
A
B
Shooting punctually, Levill by a dispart 206. Paces.
D
C
The mixt or Crooked Motion.
The violent Motion.
The naturall Motion.
B
S
900
800
700
600
500
400
300
200
100 Paces.
100
C
A
Book:V:page.68:69.
b

This 1669 artwork of missile trajectories shows the path of cannons fired at different heights. Royal Astronomical Society/Science Source

conic sections in terms of their projections. Its value was not fully appreciated until the 19th century. The study of probability as related to games of chance had also begun.

The greatest achievement of the century was the discovery of methods that applied mathematics to the study of motion. An example is Galileo's analysis of the parabolic path of projectiles, published in 1638. At the same time, the Dutch mathematician Christiaan Huygens was publishing works on the analysis of conic sections and special curves. He also presented theorems related to the paths of quickest descent of falling objects.

The unsurpassed master of the application of mathematics to problems of physics was Isaac Newton, who used analytic geometry, infinite series, and calculus to make numerous mathematical discoveries. Newton also developed his method of fluxions and fluents—the differential and integral calculus. He showed that the two methods—derivatives and integrals—were inversely related to one another. Newton and Leibniz were studying similar problems of physics and mathematics at the same

Dutch astronomer, mathematician, and physicist Christiaan Huygens developed the wave theory of light and made contributions to the science of dynamics. Courtesy of the Collection Haags Gemeentemuseum, The Hague

time. Having made his own discovery of the calculus in 1674, Leibniz published a rather obscure version of his methods in 1684, some years before Newton published a full version of his own methods. The sequence of mathematical developments that flows out of the discovery of the calculus is called analysis.

Although the new calculus was an immediate success, its methods were sharply criticized because infinitesimals were sometimes treated as if they were finite and, at other times, as if they were zero. Doubts about the foundations of the calculus were unresolved until the 19th century.

MATHEMATICS FROM THE 18TH CENTURY TO MODERN TIMES

Jakob Bernoulli, a Swiss mathematician, is best known for his work on the theory of probability. Courtesy of the Oeffentliche Bibliothek der Universität, Basel, Switz.

The discovery of analytic geometry and invention of the calculus made possible the application of mathematics to a wide range of problems in the 18th century. The Bernoullis, a Swiss family of mathematicians, were pioneers in the application of the calculus to physics. However, they were not the only ones

Johann Bernoulli contributed to the theory of differential equations. Courtesy of the Oeffentliche Bibliothek der Universität, Basel, Switz.

to advance the calculus in the 18th century. Mathematicians in France and England also tried to extend the range of the work of Newton and Leibniz.

THE 18TH CENTURY

The greatest development of mathematics in the 18th century took place on the Continent, where monarchs such as Louis XIV, Frederick the Great, and the Empress Catherine the Great of Russia provided generous support for science, including mathematics. The most prolific 18th-century mathematician was Leonhard Euler of Switzerland. He published hundreds of research papers, and his major books dealt with both the differential

Many of the great minds of Europe were drawn to the court of Empress Catherine of Russia, also called Catherine the Great. Imagno/Hulton Archive/Getty Images

BENJAMIN BANNEKER

Born near Baltimore, Md., on Nov. 9, 1731, Benjamin Banneker was the son of a slave and a free black woman. He grew up as a free black, and while attending school he demonstrated early mathematical ability. His natural childhood curiosity led him to explore a wide variety of other subjects in books he borrowed from a white neighbor.

In about 1771 Banneker began making calculations in the field of astronomy. In the science of astronomy Banneker was entirely self–taught. He accurately predicted a solar eclipse in 1789. In 1790 he was appointed to the District of Columbia Commission by President George Washington and worked with Pierre L'Enfant to plan the new capital of Washington, D.C.

Surveyor, inventor, and astronomer Benjamin Banneker is shown with a map (right) of the city of Washington. Buyenlarge/Archive Photos/Getty Images

After L'Enfant was dismissed from the project and took his detailed maps away with him, Banneker was able to reproduce them from memory. A year later he began publishing the *Pennsylvania, Delaware, Maryland, and Virginia Almanac and Ephemeris* and continued doing so until 1802. He sent the first copy of his almanac to Thomas Jefferson, then secretary of state, accompanied by a letter in which he expressed his strong feelings against slavery and praised the intellectual equality of blacks. Banneker died in Baltimore County, Md., in 1806.

and integral infinitesimal calculus as well as with algebra, geometry, mechanics, and the calculus of variations.

Joseph-Louis Lagrange contributed to mechanics, foundations of the calculus, the calculus of variations, probability theory, and the theories of numbers and equations. While analysis was being developed by some French mathematicians, others were turning to geometry and probability theory. The French astronomer Pierre-Simon Laplace succeeded in applying probability theory and analysis to the Newtonian theory of celestial mechanics. He was thereby able to establish the dynamic stability of the solar system.

THE 19TH CENTURY

The famous Greek geometer Euclid discovered important properties of numbers through a study of geometry. For example, the truth of the sentence $2 \cdot (3 + 4) = (2 \cdot 3) + (2 \cdot 4)$ is verified geometrically by noting that the area of the following rectangle:

$$\text{area} = 2 \cdot (3 + 4)$$
$$= 2 \cdot 7$$
$$= 14$$

is the same as the sum of the areas of the following rectangles:

$$\text{area} = 2 \cdot 3$$
$$= 6$$

$$\text{area} = 2 \cdot 4$$
$$= 8 \qquad [6 + 8 = 14]$$

The 19th century witnessed tremendous change in mathematics with increased specialization and new theories of algebra and number theory. The entire scope of mathematics was enriched by the discovery of controversial areas of study such as non-Euclidean geometries and transfinite set theory. Non-Euclidean geometries, in showing that consistent geometries could be developed for which Euclid's parallel postulate did not hold, raised significant questions pertaining to the foundation of mathematics.

In Germany, Carl Friedrich Gauss discovered the law of quadratic reciprocity, proved the fundamental theorem of algebra, and developed the theory of complex numbers. The Norwegian mathematician Niels Henrik Abel also made great strides during the 19th century, particularly with his theory of integrals of algebraic functions and a theorem that led to the Abelian functions, later advanced by Karl Gustav Jacobi.

The German mathematician Karl Weierstrass brought new levels of rigor to analysis by reducing its elements to arithmetic principles and by using power series as a foundation for the theory of complex functions. August Möbius, also from Germany,

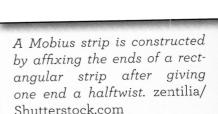

A Mobius strip is constructed by affixing the ends of a rectangular strip after giving one end a halftwist. zentilia/ Shutterstock.com

worked in the area of analytic geometry and was a pioneer in topology. He discovered the Möbius strip, a topological space obtained by twisting one end of a rectangular strip and pasting it to the other.

Mathematicians in England slowly began to take an interest in advances made on the Continent during the previous century. The Analytic Society was formed in 1812 to promote the new notation and ideas of the calculus

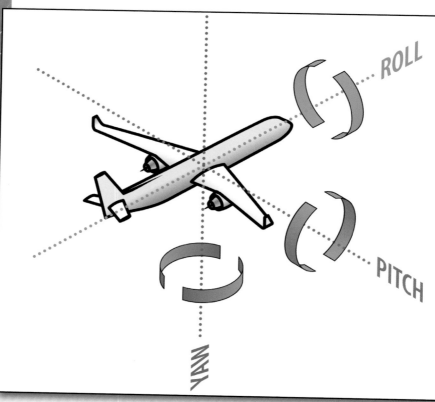

In three-dimensional space there are three axes of movement: roll, yaw, and pitch. Photo Researchers/Science Source/Getty Images

commonly used by the French. A form of non-commutative algebra called quaternions was discovered by William Rowan Hamilton, and other mathematical forms were applied to the theory of electromagnetism.

In the United States indigenous groups of mathematicians were beginning to form, particularly in the areas of linear associative algebra and logic. In France mathematicians made significant contributions to work in geometry and analysis, especially analysis of elliptic functions. Other advances were made in complex analysis, modular functions, number theory, and invariant theory. Augustin-Louis Cauchy advanced nearly every branch of mathematics, but especially real and complex analysis. Henri Poincaré made significant contributions to mathematical physics, automorphic functions, differential equations, topology, probability theory, and the foundations of mathematics. Italian mathematics in the 19th century tended to stress geometry and analysis.

Two related areas of mathematics established in the 19th century proved to be of major significance in the 20th century: set theory and mathematical logic. These were closely related to questions concerning the foundations of mathematics and the continuum of real numbers as investigated by Richard Dedekind and Georg Cantor. It was Cantor who created set theory and the theory of transfinite numbers.

MODERN TIMES

Modern mathematics is highly specialized and abstract. The advance of set theory and discoveries involving infinite sets, transfinite numbers, and purely logical paradoxes caused much concern as to the foundations of mathematics. In addition to purely theoretical developments, devices such as high-speed computers influenced both the content and the teaching of mathematics. Among the areas of mathematical research that were developed since the 20th century are abstract algebra, non-Euclidean geometry, abstract analysis, mathematical logic, and the foundations of mathematics.

Modern abstract algebra includes the study of groups, rings, algebras, lattices, and a host of other subjects developed from a formal, abstract point of view. This approach formed the cornerstone of the work of a group of mathematicians called Bourbaki. Bourbaki

Mathematician Emmy Noether did groundbreaking work in abstract algebra. She was called the best woman mathematician of the 19th century.
SPL/Science Source

used abstract algebra in an axiomatic framework to develop virtually all branches of higher mathematics, including set theory, algebra, and general topology.

The significance of non-Euclidean geometry was realized early in the 20th century when the geometry was applied in mathematical physics. It has come to play an essential role in the theory of relativity and has also raised controversial philosophical questions about the nature of mathematics and its foundations.

Another area of mathematics, abstract analysis, has produced theories of the derivatives and integrals in abstract and infinite-dimensional spaces. There are many areas of special interest in the field of abstract analysis, including functional analysis, harmonic analysis, families of functions, integral equations, divergent and asymptotic series, summability, and the study of functions of a complex variable. In recent years, analysis has advanced with the introduction of nonstandard analysis. By developing infinitesimals this theory provides an alternative to the traditional approach of using limits in the calculus.

The most notable development in the area of logic began in the 20th century with the work of two English logicians and philosophers, Bertrand Russell and Alfred North Whitehead. The object of their three-volume publication, *Principia Mathematica* (1910–13), was to show that mathematics can be deduced from a very small number of logical principles. In the 1930s questions about the logical consistency and completeness of axiomatic systems helped to spark interest in mathematical logic and concern for the foundations of mathematics. Since the 1940s mathematical logic has become increasingly specialized.

The foundations of mathematics have many "schools." At the beginning of the 20th century, David Hilbert was determined to preserve the powerful methods of transfinite set theory and the use of the infinite in mathematics, despite apparent paradoxes and numerous objections. He believed it was possible to find finite means of establishing the truth of mathematical propositions, even when the infinite was involved. To this end Hilbert devoted considerable effort to developing a metamathematical theory of proofs. His program was virtually abandoned in the 1930s when Kurt Gödel demonstrated that for any general axiomatic system there are always theorems that cannot be proved or disproved.

Gödel's proof, which stated that the basic axioms of arithmetic may give rise to contradictions, became a hallmark of 20th-century mathematics. Alfred Eisenstaedt/The LIFE Picture Collection/Getty Images

Hilbert's followers, known as formalists, view mathematics in terms of abstract structures. The axioms are developed as arbitrary rules. When applied to the unspecified elements of the theory, they can be used to establish the validity of theorems. Mathematical "truth" is thus reduced to the question of logical self-consistency. Those opposed to the formalist view, called intuitionists, believe that the basic truths of mathematics present themselves as fundamental intuitions of thought. The oldest philosophy of mathematics is usually ascribed to Plato. Platonism asserts the existence of eternal truths, independent of the human mind. In this philosophy the truths of mathematics arise from an abstract, ideal reality.

THE STUDY OF QUANTITY, MAGNITUDE, AND RELATIONS OF NUMBERS AND SYMBOLS

Throughout history, mathematics has become increasingly complex and diversified. At the same time, however, it has become increasingly general and abstract. There are several major subdivisions of modern mathematics, including arithmetic, algebra, geometry, trigonometry, calculus, and various forms of mathematical theory.

ARITHMETIC

Arithmetic comes from the word *arithmos*, meaning "number" in Greek. It is the study of the nature and properties of numbers. It includes study of the algorithms of calculation with numbers, namely the basic operations of addition, subtraction, multiplication, and division, as well as the taking of powers and roots. Arithmetic is often applied in the calculation of fractions, ratios, percentages, and proportions.

ALGEBRA

Algebra has often been described as "arithmetic with letters." Unlike arithmetic, which deals with specific numbers, algebra introduces variables that greatly extend the generality and scope of arithmetic.

1. $Y - 5 + 4$

2. $3 \times A = 12$

3. $K \div 3 = 4$

4. $M/4 = 3$

47

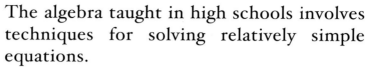

The algebra taught in high schools involves techniques for solving relatively simple equations.

Modern algebra, or abstract algebra, is a more general branch of mathematics that analyzes algebraic axioms and operations with arbitrary sets of symbols. Special areas of abstract algebra include the study of groups, rings, fields, the algebra of matrices, and a large variety of nonassociative and noncommutative algebras. Special algebras of sets and vectors and Boolean algebras arise in the study of logic. Algebra is used in the calculation of compound interest, in the solution of distance-rate-time problems, or in any situation in the sciences where the determination of unknown quantities from a body of known data is required.

GEOMETRY

The word *geometry* is derived from the Greek meaning "earth measurement." Although geometry originated for practical purposes in ancient Egypt and Babylonia, the Greeks investigated it in a more systematic and general way.

In the 19th century, Euclidean geometry's status as the primary geometry was challenged by the discovery of non-Euclidean geometries. These inspired a new approach to the subject by presenting theorems in terms of axioms applied to properties assigned to undefined elements called points and lines. This led to many new geometries, including elliptical, hyperbolic, and parabolic geometries. Modern abstract geometry deals with very general questions of space, shape, size, and other properties

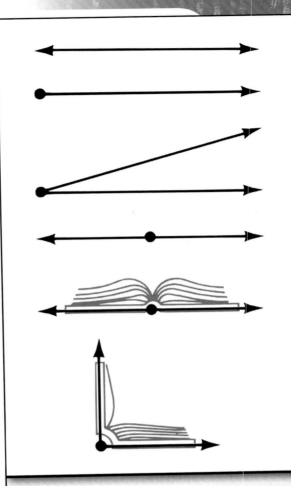

Some geometric figures are (from top): a line, a ray, an angle, and a straight angle. The latter two are also shown as an open book. Encyclopædia Britannica, Inc.

of figures. Projective geometry, for example, is an abstract geometry concerned with the geometric properties that remain invariant under the projection of figures onto other figures, as in the case of mathematical perspective.

A very useful approach to geometry is found in topology, the study of the properties of a geometric figure that remain the same when a figure is subjected to continuous transformation without loss of identity of any of its parts. Differential geometry is the study of geometry in terms of infinitesimals.

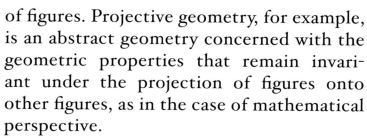

Geometry	Algebra
A point	(x,y)
Distance between two points	$\sqrt{(x_2-x_1)^2+(y_2-y_1)^2}$
Slope of a line segment	$\dfrac{y_2-y_1}{x_2-x_1}$ or $\tan\theta$
Line through a given point and with a given slope	$y-y_1=m(x-x_1)$
Line through two given points	$\dfrac{y-y_1}{x-x_1}=\dfrac{y_2-y_1}{x_2-x_1}$

ANALYTIC GEOMETRY AND TRIGONOMETRY

Analytic geometry combines the generality of algebra with the precision of geometry. It is sometimes called Cartesian geometry, after Descartes, who was the first to exploit the methods of algebra in geometry. Analytic geometry addresses geometric problems from an algebraic point of view by associating any curve with variables by means of a coordinate system. For example, in a two-dimensional coordinate system, any point on a curve can be associated with a pair of points (a,b). General properties of such curves can then be studied in terms of their algebraic properties.

Trigonometry is the study of triangles, angles, and their relations. It also involves the study of trigonometric functions. There are six trigonometric ratios associated with an angle: sine, cosine, tangent, cotangent, secant, and cosecant. These are especially useful in determining unknown angles or the sides of triangles based upon known trigonometric ratios. In antiquity, trigonometry was used with considerable success by surveyors and astronomers.

Gottfried Wilhelm Leibniz was regarded as a genius in the same way as Leonardo da Vinci, with one difference: he was not an artist. Leemage/ Universal Images Group/Getty Images

CALCULUS

The calculus discovered in the 17th century by Newton and Leibniz used infinitesimal quantities to determine tangents to curves and to facilitate calculation of lengths and areas of curved figures. These operations were found to be inversely related. Newton called them "fluxions" and "fluents," corresponding to what are now termed derivatives and integrals. Leibniz called them "differences" and "sums."

In the 19th century, in response to questions about its rigorous foundations, the calculus was developed in terms of a theory of limits. Analysis—differential and integral calculus—was subsequently approached even more rigorously by those who sought to establish its results by strictly arithmetic means. This required an exact definition of the continuity of the real numbers. Others extended the power of analysis with very general theories of measure.

Analysis gives primary emphasis to functions, convergence of sequences, series, continuity, differentiability, and questions about the completeness of the real numbers.

Introductory courses in calculus generally include study of logarithms, exponential functions, trigonometric functions, and transcendental functions.

COMPLEX ANALYSIS

Complex analysis extends the methods of analysis from real to complex variables. Complex numbers first arose to permit general solutions to algebraic equations. They take the form $a + bi$, where a and b are real numbers. The variable a is called the real part of the number; b, the imaginary part of the number; and i represents the complex, or "imaginary," number signified by the square root of -1. Because complex numbers have two independent components, a and b, they are especially useful in applications whenever two variables must be treated simultaneously. For example, complex analysis has proved particularly

valuable in applications to fluid dynamics, where both pressure and velocity vary from point to point. Complex numbers were made more acceptable to many in the 19th century when they were given a geometric interpretation.

Sir Isaac Newton was a physicist and mathematician who formulated three fundamental laws of motion and developed the law of gravitation.
Dorling Kindersley/Getty Images

NUMBER THEORY

It has been said that any unsolved mathematical problem that is over a century old and is still considered interesting belongs to number theory. This branch of mathematics involves the study of the properties of numbers and the structure of different number systems. It is concerned with integers, or whole numbers. Many problems in number theory deal with prime numbers. These are integers larger than 1 that have only themselves and 1 as factors.

Questions about highest common factors, least common multiples, decompositions into primes, and the representation of natural numbers in certain forms as well as their divisibility are all the province of number theory. Computers have recently been applied to the solution of certain number-theory problems.

PROBABILITY THEORY AND STATISTICS

The branch of mathematics concerned with the analysis of random phenomena is called probability theory. The entire set of possible outcomes of a random event is called the sample space. Each outcome in this space is assigned a probability, a number indicating the likelihood that the particular event will arise in a single instance. An example of a random experiment is the tossing of a coin. The sample space consists of the two outcomes, heads or tails, and the probability assigned to each is one half.

Statistics applies probability theory to real cases and involves the analysis of empirical data. The word *statistics* reflects the original application of mathematical methods to data collected for purposes of the state. Such studies led to general techniques for analyzing data and computing various values, drawing correlations, using methods of sampling, counting, estimating, and ranking data according to certain criteria.

SET THEORY

Created in the 19th century by the German mathematician Georg Cantor, set theory was originally meant to provide techniques for the mathematical analysis of the infinite. Set theory deals with the properties of well-defined collections of objects. Sets may be

Modern mathematical analysis is based on Georg Cantor's theory of sets. Emilio Segrè Visual Archives/American Institute of Physics/ Science Source

finite or infinite. A finite set has a definite number of members; such a set might consist of all the integers from 1 to 1,000. An infinite set has an endless number of members. For example, all of the positive integers compose an infinite set.

Cantor developed a theory of infinite numbers and transfinite arithmetic to go along with them. His continuum hypothesis conjectures that the set of all real numbers is the second smallest infinite set. The smallest infinite set is composed of the integers or any set equivalent to it.

Early in the 20th century certain contradictions of set theory concerning infinite sets, transfinite numbers, and purely logical paradoxes brought about attempts to axiomatize set theory in hopes of eliminating such difficulties. When Kurt Gödel showed that for any axiomatic system propositions could be devised that were neither true nor false, it seemed that the traditional certainty of mathematics had been suddenly lost.

In the 1960s Paul Cohen succeeded in showing the independence of the continuum hypothesis, namely that it could be neither proved nor disproved within a given axiomatization of set theory. This meant that it was

GEORG CANTOR

Georg Ferdinand Ludwig Philipp Cantor was born on March 3, 1845, in St. Petersburg, Russia. In 1856 the Cantor family moved to Frankfurt am Main, Germany Before Georg was 15 years old, his talent for mathematics became evident. Choosing a career as a mathematician, he studied at the universities of Zürich, Berlin, and Göttingen. He received a doctoral degree in 1867. He taught at a girls' school in Berlin, then in 1869 joined the faculty of the University of Halle in eastern Germany. The salary he earned there was never great, but he inherited enough money from his father to build a comfortable house for himself and his family.

From about 1884 until he died Cantor suffered occasional mental illness. Persons familiar with his life have suggested that these attacks were brought on by the difficulty of his research and by the unwillingness of other mathematicians (Leopold Kronecker, in particular) to accept his unusual results. Cantor died on Jan. 6, 1918, in the psychiatric institute at Halle. Cantor founded the theory of sets and introduced the concept of transfinite numbers. Both are used in studying different classes of things too numerous to count, such as the natural numbers (1, 2, 3, ...) or the points on a line. All branches of mathematics use the concept of the set.

possible to contemplate non-Cantorian set theories in which the continuum hypothesis might be negated, much as non-Euclidean geometries treat geometry without assuming the necessary validity of Euclid's parallel postulate.

LOGIC

Logic is the study of the way in which valid conclusions may be drawn from given premises. It was first treated systematically by Aristotle and later developed in terms of an algebra of logic. Symbolic logic arose from traditional logic by using symbols to stand for propositions and relations between them. Modern logicians use algebraic and formal methods to study the relations between logical propositions. This has led to model theory and model logic.

Just like a language, mathematics has evolved and changed over time. Mathematics started in the ancient world because people needed a way to measure time and count. Early evidence of how numbers were used can be found on ancient cave walls and pottery.

Mathematics developed with each century and the specific needs of each culture. Asian civilizations began to create sophisticated number systems. The Egyptians showed knowledge of geometry as they built the pyramids. The Greeks advanced reasoning. The Indians advanced algebra. The Germans, English, and French helped math become specialized.

Mathematics in the ancient world is nothing like mathematics in modern society. Today, math is highly specialized and includes the subjects of arithmetic, geometry, algebra, calculus, probability, and statistics. There are two major divisions of mathematics: pure and applied. Mathematics is everywhere and used by people dozens of times a day. Mathematicians work in every area of society. Today's society couldn't function without math. Imagine how math will continue to evolve in the future. The possibilities are endless.

asymptotic The relation of a line or curve to another line or curve that acts as its limit, such as a descending curve that approaches but does not reach the horizontal axis.

axiomatic Based on or involving a rule or principle that is accepted as true.

coin To create a word or phrase that is used by others.

deductive Using logic or reason to form a conclusion or opinion about something.

derivative Something that comes from or is formed from something else.

dimension Measurement in one of three coordinates that determine a position in space or in one of four coordinates that determine a position in space and time.

estimating Judging tentatively or approximately the value, worth, or significance of something.

hypothesis An idea or theory that is not proved but that leads to further study or discussion.

integral The inverse of derivative.

magnitude A spatial quality such as size, quantity, or number.

mina An ancient unit of weight with a value equal to 1/60 of a talent.

papyrus Paper made from the papyrus plant that was used in ancient times.

paradox Something (such as a situation) made up of two opposite things that seems impossible but is actually true or possible.

pervasive Existing in every part of something.

properties The qualities or characteristics of something.

quantity An amount or number of something.

ranking The position relative to others in a group.

rigorous Very strict and demanding.

sexagesimal Of or relating to the number 60.

shekel Ancient unit of weight, especially a Hebrew unit.

summability Capable of being added.

surveying A branch of mathematics concerned with determining the area of any portion of the Earth's surface.

talent An ancient unit of weight.

theorem A formula or statement that can be proved from other formulas or statements.

American Mathematical Society (AMS)
201 Charles Street
Providence, RI 02904-2294
(800) 321-4AMS (4267)
Website: http://www.ams.org
The AMS was founded in 1888 to promote
mathematical research, support mathematics education, and advance the status of the
mathematics profession.

Canadian Mathematical Society
209-1725 St. Laurent Boulevard
Ottawa, ON K1G 3V4
Canada
(613) 733-2662
Website: http://cms.math.ca
This organization was founded in 1945 to
develop partnerships with users of mathematics in industry and education, as well as
other mathematical associations, in order to
strengthen mathematics in Canada.

Kappa Mu Epsilon (KME)
The American Statistical Association
Attn: Rhonda McKee
University of Central Missouri
Warrensburg, MO 64093

Website: http://www.kappamuepsilon.org
Founded in 1931, KME is a mathematics honor
 society that promotes mathematics among
 undergraduate students. Chapters are
 located in recognized colleges and universities with strong mathematics programs.

Mathematical Association of America
1529 18th Street NW
Washington, DC 20036-1358
(202) 387-5200
Website: http://www.maa.org
This is the largest professional society that
 focuses on undergraduate mathematics.
 Members include teachers from high school
 to the college and university level, students,
 mathematicians, and scientists. Membership
 is open open to all interested in the mathematical sciences.

Mu Alpha Theta
University of Oklahoma
601 Elm Avenue, Room 1102
Norman, OK 73019
(405) 325-4489
Website: http://www.mualphatheta.org
This national high school and two-year col-
 lege mathematics honor society has nearly

100,000 members and is involved in over 2,000 schools across the United States. The society's goal is to develop interest and scholarship in the field of mathematics.

National Council of Teachers of Mathematics (NCTM)
1906 Association Drive
Reston, VA 20191-1502
(800) 235-7566
Website: http://www.nctm.org
The NCTM is the public voice of mathematics education, supporting teachers at all levels to ensure mathematics learning of the highest quality.

WEBSITES

Because of the changing nature of Internet links, Rosen Publishing has developed an online list of websites related to the subject of this book. This site is updated regularly. Please use this link to access this list:

http://www.rosenlinks.com/TSOM/Study

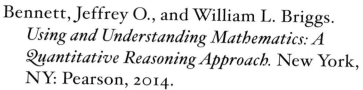

Bennett, Jeffrey O., and William L. Briggs. *Using and Understanding Mathematics: A Quantitative Reasoning Approach.* New York, NY: Pearson, 2014.

Bird, John. *Engineering Mathematics.* New York, NY: Routledge, 2014.

Dantzig, Tobias. *Number: The Language of Science.* New York, NY: Penguin, 2007.

Doxiadis, Apostolos. *Logicomix: An Epic Search for Truth.* New York, NY: Bloomsbury, 2009.

Ellenberg, Jordan. *How Not to Be Wrong: The Power of Mathematical Thinking.* New York, NY: Penguin, 2014.

Gregersen, Erik, ed. *The Britannica Guide to the History of Mathematics.* New York, NY: Rosen Educational Services, 2010.

Harmon, Daniel E. *Internship and Volunteer Opportunities for Science and Math Wizards.* New York, NY: Rosen Publishing, 2012.

Lockhart, Paul. *Measurement.* Cambridge, MA: Harvard University Press, 2012.

Miller, Julie, Molly O'Neill, and Nancy Hyde. *Basic College Mathematics.* New York, NY: McGraw-Hill Science, 2014.

Oakley, Barbara. *A Mind for Numbers: How to Excel at Math and Science (Even If*

You Flunked Algebra). New York, NY: Tarcher, 2014.

Pickover, Clifford A. *The Math Book: From Pythagoras to the 57th Dimension, 250 Milestones in the History of Mathematics.* New York, NY: Sterling, 2009.

Pitici, Mircea, ed. *The Best Writing on Mathematics 2013.* Princeton, NJ: Princeton University Press, 2014.

A

Abel, Niels Henrik, 37
algebra, 8, 9, 10, 11, 15, 16, 18,
    21, 22, 24, 25, 35, 36, 39, 62
  abstract, 40, 42, 48
  described, 47–48
  fundamental theorem
    of, 37
  linear associative, 39
  origin of name, 24
analysis, 30, 35, 37, 39, 53
  abstract, 40, 42
  complex, 9, 54–55
  nonstandard, 42
Analytic Society, 38–39
Apollonius of Perga, 18–19,
    20, 23
applied mathematics, 10, 62
Arabs, early, 20, 21, 23, 24
Archimedes, 18–19, 23
Aristotle, 18, 61
arithmetic, 10, 22, 24
  described, 47
  transfinite, 59
Aryabhata, 22
astronomy, and mathematics,
    20, 22, 25–26, 34, 35, 51

B

Babylonians, 8, 14–15
Banneker, Benjamin, 34–35
base-60 system, 14–15
base-10 systems, 14

Bernoulli family, 31–32
Bhaskara II, 22
Bourbaki, 40–42
Brahmagupta, 22

C

calculus, 8, 9, 10, 21, 25, 26, 28,
    30, 31, 32, 38, 42
  described, 53–54
Cantor, Georg, 40, 57, 59, 60
Cardano, Gerolamo, 25
Cauchy, Augustin-Louis, 39
Cohen, Paul, 59
complex analysis, 9
  described, 54–55
complex functions, 37
complex numbers, 37
computers, 9, 11, 40, 56
continuum hypothesis, 59–61

D

decimal system, 14, 22
Dedekind, Richard, 40
Descartes, René, 26, 51
Diophantus, 18

E

Egyptians, ancient, 8, 12–14,
    16, 62
Elements of Geometry, 16,
    19–20
Euclid, 16, 18–20, 23, 36, 37,
    49, 61
Euler, Leonhard, 32–35